Plus

Safety

in My Neighborhood

by Shelly Lyons

Consulting Editor: Gail Saunders-Smith, PhD

CAPSTONE PRESS
a capstone imprint

Pebble Plus is published by Capstone Press,
1710 Roe Crest Drive, North Mankato, Minnesota 56003.
www.capstonepub.com

Library of Congress Cataloging-in-Publication Data
Lyons, Shelly.
Safety in my neighborhood / by Shelly Lyons.
p. cm. — (Pebble plus: My Neighborhood)
ISBN 978-1-62065-102-5 (library binding)
ISBN 978-1-62065-887-1 (paperback)
ISBN 978-1-4765-1724-7 (ebook PDF)
1. Safety education—Juvenile literature. 2. Child rearing—Juvenile literature. I. Title.
HQ770.7.L96 2013
363.1—dc23   2012023421

Editorial Credits
Sarah Bennett, designer; Svetlana Zhurkin, media researcher; Kathy McColley, production specialist

Photo Credits
Capstone Studio: Karon Dubke, 7, 9, 11; iStockphotos: Agnieszka Kirinicjanow, 19, kali9, 21, Kathy Dewar, 5, Yarinca, 17, AISPIX by Image Source, 15; Shutterstock: A-R-T (background), 1 and throughout, Richard Susanto, 13, spotmatik, cover

Note to Parents and Teachers

The My Neighborhood set supports social studies standards related to community. This book describes and illustrates safety in a neighborhood. The images support early readers in understanding the text. The repetition of words and phrases helps early readers learn new words. This book also introduces early readers to subject-specific vocabulary words, which are defined in the Glossary section. Early readers may need assistance to read some words and to use the Table of Contents, Glossary, Read More, Internet Sites, and Index sections of the book.

Printed in the United States of America in North Mankato, Minnesota.
092012   006933CGS13

Table of Contents

Being Safe. 4

Pedaling Smarts. 6

Numbers and Rules 10

On Your Own. 16

Glossary 22

Read More 23

Internet Sites. 23

Index 24

Being Safe

Being safe in my neighborhood means following rules. It also means knowing the adults whom I can trust.

Pedaling Smarts

Cali rides her bike
to her friend's house.
She wears a helmet
and bright clothing.

Sid knows hand signals

for biking.

The signals warn others

when Sid is turning or stopping.

Numbers and Rules

Tyra practices dialing

her phone number.

She remembers her address.

In an emergency,

she will know these numbers.

Mark goes out to play.

He follows his parents' rules
and stays in the yard.

At the park, Gavin sees

two boys fighting.

He and his dad talk about

solving problems with words.

On Your Own

Mika walks home
from school with friends.
They stick to a route
they know well.

At the bus stop,

Alex stands in line.

He stays far from the bus

when it is moving.

The families in my neighborhood

work together to be safe.

We get to know each other.

How do you stay safe

in your neighborhood?

Glossary

address—the number and street name of a home

emergency—a sudden and dangerous situation that must be handled quickly

hand signal—a hand sign that stands for a word

helmet—a hard hat that protects the head

neighborhood—a small area in a town or city where people live

route—the road or course followed to get somewhere

Read More

Guard, Anara. *What If a Stranger Approaches You?* Danger Zone. Mankato, Minn.: Picture Window Books, 2012.

Rau, Dana Meachen. *Safety at Home*. Safe Kids. New York: Marshall Cavendish Benchmark, 2010.

Weber, Rebecca. *Safety Basics*. Health and Your Body. North Mankato, Minn.: Capstone Press, 2012.

Internet Sites

FactHound offers a safe, fun way to find Internet sites related to this book. All of the sites on FactHound have been researched by our staff.

Here's all you do:

Visit *www.facthound.com*

Type in this code: 9781620651025

Super-cool stuff! Check out projects, games and lots more at www.capstonekids.com

Index

addresses, 10

bike safety, 6, 8

bus stop safety, 18

emergencies, 10

following rules, 4, 12

getting to know people, 20

phone numbers, 10

solving disagreements, 14

walking home from school, 16

Word Count: 157
Grade: 1
Early-Intervention Level: 17